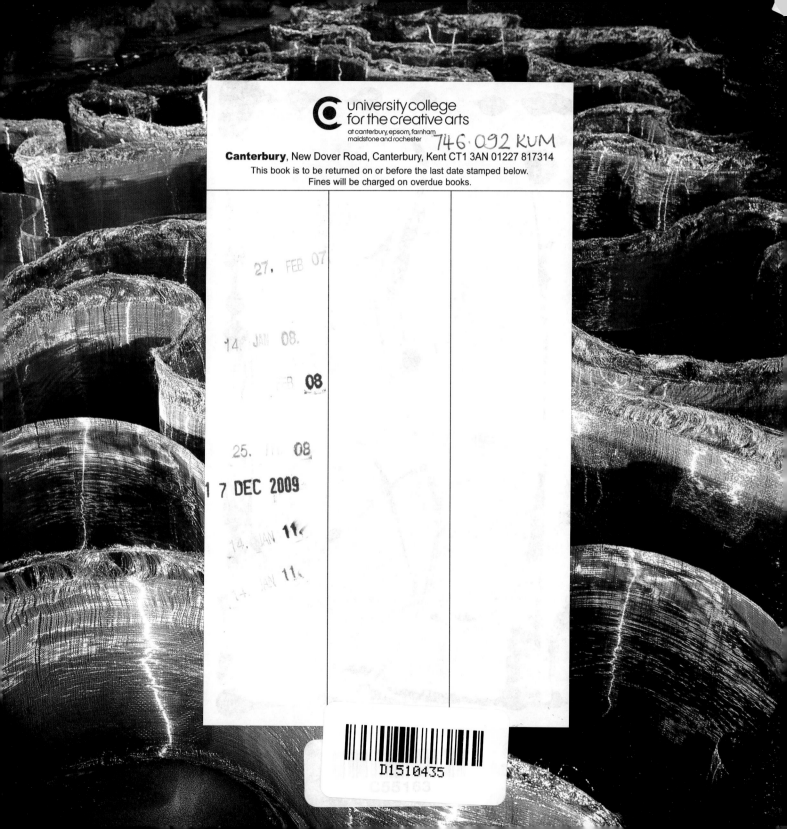

Art © Kyoko Kumai
Author: Ryoko Kuroda
Series Editor: Matthew Koumis
Graphic Design: Rachael Dadd & MK
Reprographics: Ermanno Beverari
Printed in Italy by Grafiche AZ

© Telos Art Publishing 2003

Telos Art Publishing
PO Box 125, Winchester
SO23 7UJ England
T +44 (0) 1962 864546
F +44 (0) 1962 864727
E editorial@telos.net
E sales@telos.net
W www.telos.net

ISBN 1 902015 65 7 (softback)

A CIP catalogue record for this book is
available from The British Library

Notes

All dimensions are shown in imperial
and metric, height x width x depth.
All work is in private collections unless
otherwise stated.

Photo Credits

Hiroshi Narita, Hiroyuki Hirai, Junichi
Ochiai, Mitsumasa Fijitsuka, Ittetsu
Futatsuka, Tadahisa Sakurai, Takashi
Hatakeyama, Takeo Ishimatsu, Yoshinori
Takeuchi, Yozo Fujita

Publisher's Acknowledgements

Thanks to Keiko Kawashima of Kyoto
International Contemporary Textile Arts
Centre; Paul Richardson of Oxford Brookes
University; Simon Stokes of Tarlo Lyons;
John Denison, Leo Pickford, Agostini
Alessandra, Crivelli Simone, Valle Marco,
Dò Moreno.

front cover illustration:
Frozen Wind
1985-1987
stainless steel filament
4.2 x 32 x 32ft (1.3 x 10 x 10m)

back cover illustration:
Windy Earth in the Night
1990
stainless steel filament
3.2 x 32 x 64ft (1 x 10 x 20m)
Installation at Ohara-Ryu Kaikan, Tokyo

Illustrations on page 1 and 48:
The Air '85
1985
stainless steel filament
22 x 32 x 32ft (7 x 10 x 10m)

portfolio collection
Kyoko Kumai

TELOS

Contents

6   Foreword
by **Martina Margetts**

11   Wind Blowing Through Future Space,
The World of Kyoko Kumai
by **Ryoko Kuroda**

23   Japanese translation

31   Colour Plates

44   Biography

Blowing in the Wind
1988
stainless steel filament
8 x 8 x 8in (20 x 20 x 20cm)
Collection of Victoria & Albert Museum, London;
Montréal Decorative Art Museum;
Savaria Museum, Hungary

Foreword

Pass of the Coloured Wind
1975
wool thread, wooden frame
7.4 x 8.7 x 2.6ft (2.3 x 2.7 x 0.8m)

The West has consistently admired the development of Japanese textile art in recent decades and Kyoko Kumai plays a central role, as artist, teacher, adviser. The consummate poetry of her vision has given the world some astonishing evocations of nature. The traditions of weaving and of working by hand rather than machine or computer lie at the root of Kyoko Kumai's procedures, but her use of industrial material and off-loom three-dimensional composition places her work firmly in the arena of modern art. As an exhibitor at Lausanne and prizewinner at Kyoto and Lodz, as the recipient of over fifty major commissions and exhibitor at such distinguished and diverse institutions as the Museum of Modern Art, New York and Science Museum,

London, Kyoko Kumai already has an international following, but I am delighted that this monograph will bring her even wider recognition and allow the full range of her achievement to be considered in detail.

Kyoko Kumai reveals a quintessentially Japanese sensibility in her art, putting feeling before theory. As Soetsu Yanagi wrote in *The Unknown Craftsman: a Japanese Insight into Beauty*: "One cannot produce intuition out of knowledge. Thus the basis of aesthetics must not be intellectual concepts". Drawing on observation and on childhood memory of nature's elements – wind, fire, air, earth – Kyoko Kumai enables us to participate directly in her lived experience. While some works are small and intimate,

her formidable reputation rests on her vast works which suggest growth in nature, spreading across walls and floors, atmospherically enveloping space and light and suggesting a cyclical rather than linear shape of time. Pattern, colour, form, as well as monumentality and lightness (permanence and transience), are all derived from the patient and repetitive manipulation of stainless-steel filament; but while the economy of material and process suggests a minimalist approach, it belies a lingering emotional charge.

Martina Margetts
Senior Tutor in Critical
and Historical Studies
Royal College of Art, London

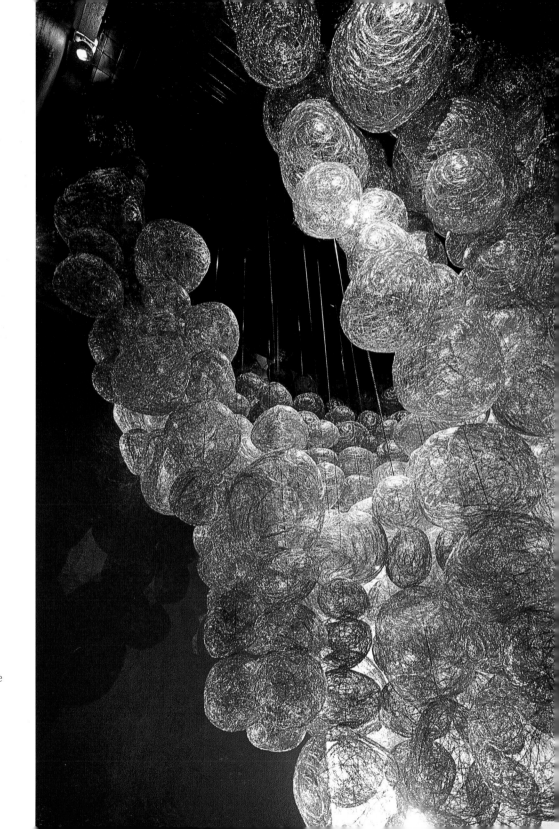

right:
Sen Man Na Yu Ta
1995
stainless steel filament
14.4 x 14.4 x 14.4ft (4.5 x 4.5 x 4.5m)
Collection of Tenkai-kutsu Mandera-yuen
Tateyama Toyama
(Architect: Kijo Rokkaku)

left:
Sen Man Na Yu Ta
1992
stainless steel filament, stainless steel pole
9.6 x 3.8 x 3.8ft (3 x 1.2 x 1.2m)

Wind Blowing Through Future Space

The World of Kyoko Kumai

Ryoko Kuroda

Art Historian and Art Critic

The Wind Blowing Over the Grass
1999
stainless steel filament
1 x 14 x 14ft (0.3 x 4.5 x 4.5m)

The Museum of Contemporary Art, Gunma, located in the city of Takasaki, 100 kilometers to the north of Tokyo, has a new contemporary wing designed by Arata Isozaki. This building contains three galleries. They are all designed with great simplicity but each has a different atmosphere with a stimulating effect on the imagination. Entering these rooms, one feels a slight tension in the air and a sense of being in a futuristic space never experienced before. One of the works of art installed here is Kyoko Kumai's *Air Cube*. The room around it is dimly lighted but the work itself is illuminated with a faint light and seems to be alive and breathing in the elegant and innovative space. It looks as if streams of air have suddenly turned into fine, glowing lines and come together to form a three dimensional object. *Air Cube* is strong but delicate, substantial but about to melt away. The air seems to condense in places and blow lightly through the form, turning into mist in its upper regions, rising up, and disappearing into the surrounding air. The space now belongs to the artist and is pervaded by a glorious sense of tranquility. Standing in the space, I feel a nostalgic peace but also a great excitement, as if touched by a wind blowing through future space.

Kumai's art, exemplified by this work, concentrates on the expression of light and atmosphere. She reports that her art is inspired by a primal experience of seeing a gust of wind blow through a rice field, making a path between the stalks, and she was greatly moved by this vision of the breath of nature. Kumai speaks simply and gently about her approach to making art. "I want to make things that I want to see, things I have never seen." Her words remind me of a statement by the poet So Sakon on poetry: "Poetry is the desire to see the invisible, hear the inaudible, touch the untouchable, smell what cannot be smelled, taste what cannot be tasted, feel things that cannot be felt, and make absent things present."

Air Cube
1996
stainless steel filament
4 x 5 x 5ft (1.2 x 1.5 x 1.5m)
Collection of the Museum of Contemporary Art, Gunma, Japan

This statement could apply to everything called art, including poetry, music, and the visual arts. It is not a simple matter to give form to desire. Innumerable poets, musicians, and artists undergo great suffering and anguish as they cultivate their minds, replenish the springs of the heart, and patiently search by trial and error for a means of expression. Only those who have obtained their own personal form of expression are privileged to realize their dreams.

Kumai obtained this privilege when she actively chose stainless steel filaments as the material to carry her dreams. After graduating in visual design from Tokyo National University of Fine Arts and Music in 1983, she studied weaving on her own and won the New Artist's Prize at the 'Japan Craft Design Exhibition' with a richly colored three-dimensional piece of fiber art. This three-dimensional form made of highly plastic woven fabric incorporated air in its warp and woof and floated in mid-air, showing that her heart was already captured by the possibilities of expressing atmospheric qualities. Because fabric is so flexible, it cannot escape the effects of gravity, and this puts some restrictions on form. Fibrous materials are used to cover and decorate our bodies and give color to our lives, so they have immediate associations of warmth and comfort, but it is more difficult to use them to express the exhilaration and excitement of wind and air that inspired Kumai. She wanted to make woven fabrics independent of gravity, tough but delicate textiles that electrify the atmosphere and stir up the breath of wind in space.

Legacy of Wind
1984
wool thread, stainless steel filament
7.4 x 12.8 x 1ft (2.3 x 4 x 0.3m)

Blowing in the Wind

1985-1987

stainless steel filament, cotton thread

7.4 x 32 x 1ft (2.3 x 10 x 0.3m)

13th International Biennial, Lausanne

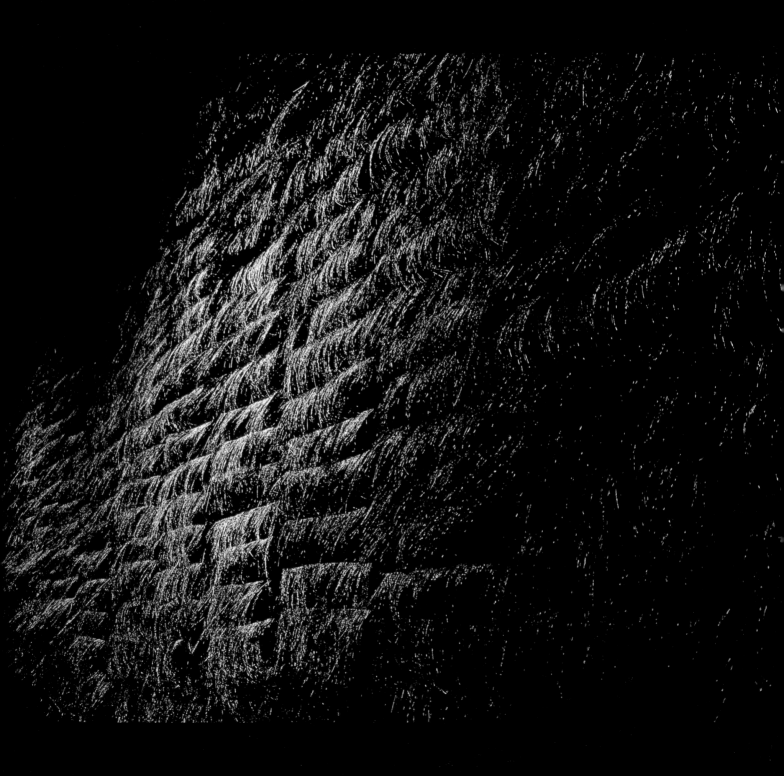

At this stage Kumai introduced stainless steel filaments as the warp of the fabric to provide support and liberate the form from gravity, bringing air movements into her art like the breath of life and allowing it to jump out into space. With these materials, she created a wind that began blowing through space. However, she found it difficult to express the view of nature that had been deeply and delicately impressed upon her mind with conventional materials and weaving techniques. Eventually, the stainless steel filaments began to take a more open role as an important part of her artistic vocabulary, essential to conveying her desires. Around 1985 they were used as both warp and woof of a glittering stainless steel fabric that began to move away from the loom.

Emotions ran through the artist's body and out her fingertips into the stainless steel filaments, directly translated into her artistic vocabulary. She had finally obtained the privilege of making dreams into reality. Just as everything that King Midas of Crete touched turned to gold, the stainless steel filaments in Kumai's hands turned into air filled with light. Her art conjures up wind, mist, rain, snow, and flame with surprising boldness and delicacy. These fine, strong filaments made of industrial stainless steel are produced with highly advanced technology. One would hardly expect them to be transformed into an expression of the world of nature, the source of our life.

I have mentioned the sense of nostalgic peace I experienced in the space around *Air Cube*. It recalled the experience of seeing the *Pine Trees* screen by Hasegawa Tohaku, a masterpiece of ink painting from the Momoyama period. The simple pictorial space of this screen is constructed entirely in gradations of black and white, showing a number of pine trees are distributed at rhythmic intervals in a vast empty space. In the infinitely expanding space, filled with misty rain, one can almost hear the low sighing of the trees.

Sen Man Na Yu Ta – Wall
1998
stainless steel filament
8 x 12.8 x 1ft (2.5 x 4 x 0.3m)
Collection of the Central Museum of Lodz, Poland

The space dominated by the glittering silver *Air Cube* is thinned or thickened in infinite variations, an effect similar to that of the *Pine Trees* screen. The work is filled with an elegant sense of tranquility that surrounds and envelops us, expressing endless space and time.

In every age, the most revolutionary works of art arise from the accumulated remains of the past. Kumai's wind is the breath of the present age but it comes out of the ancient Japanese view of nature. Her work expresses an endless faith in nature, projecting and unifying the world inside her heart and revealing the fundamental sense of beauty underlying Japanese culture, which combines elegant decorative qualities with the energy of life and a simple sense of tranquility. This is why I felt a sense of nostalgia and peace while looking at *Air Cube*.

Recently, Kumai is working on a piece entitled *Luxuriant Growth* inspired by the image of withered grass in the winter. A sense of poignant loneliness is contained in the soft light that seems to project the fading glow of ebbing life. It expresses the warm, quiet gaze of the artist, accepting human life and death within the natural environment. Kumai began her artistic career by attempting to embody her impressions of the breath of nature. Now, using a freer artistic vocabulary, she seems to be engaging the essence of the world.

Ryoko Kuroda
Art Historian
Art Critic

Screen – Sudare
1994
stainless steel filament
6.4 x 4.2ft (2 x 1.3m)

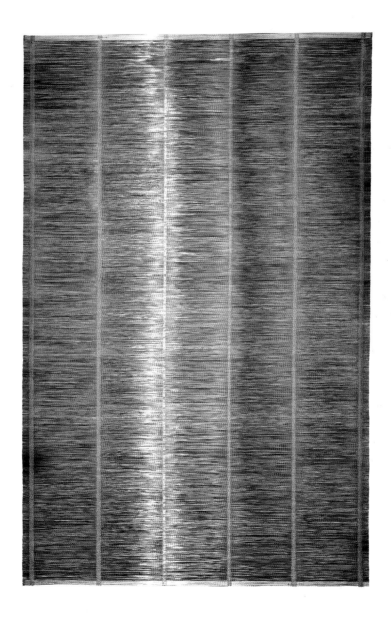

"Poetry is the desire to see the invisible, hear the inaudible, touch the untouchable, smell what cannot be smelled, taste what cannot be tasted, feel things that cannot be felt, and make absent things present."

Frozen Air
2002
stainless steel filament
8 x 41.6 x 6.4ft (2.5 x 13 x 2m)

未来空間に吹く風──熊井恭子の世界

黒田 亮子
美術史家、美術評論家

above:

Far Far Away 1980

cotton thread, gold coloured thread,

stainless steel filament

5.7 x 14.4 x 0.6ft (1.8 x 4.5 x 0.2m)

pages 24 & 25:

Frozen Wind

1985-1987

stainless steel filament

4.2 x 32 x 32ft (1.3 x 10 x 10m)

　東京から北へ100キロ離れた群馬県高崎市にある群馬県立近代美術館には、1998年、磯崎新の設計により3室からなる現代美術棟が増築された。それぞれに異なった表情を見せるが、共通するのは簡素でありながら幻想的な豊かさを内包していることであり、中に入ると、快い緊張感と共に、経験したこともない未来空間に足を踏み入れたような幻惑にとらわれる。ある時この1室の暗闇の中でかすかな光に照らされて、熊井恭子の《AIR CUBE》は、最初からその洗練された革新的な空間の中に生まれ出たように生き生きと呼吸をしていた。澄んだ大気の流れが一瞬のうちにきらめく細い線となって絡み合い立方体を形作ったかのような《AIR CUBE》は、繊細でありながら強靭であり、硬質な中にも溶けるように淡く、凝縮された空気が軽やかに作品の中を吹き抜けて、その上部から靄となって周囲の空間に立ちのぼり溶け込んでいるようだった。ここはすでに熊井の空間となり、空間全体に豪奢な静謐感が響き渡っていた。この空間の中で、私は懐かしい安らぎと共に、未来空間を吹く風にふれたようなときめきを感じた。

　熊井恭子のテーマは、この作品に見られるように、光や大気の表現に集中している。子供の頃に見た、稲穂を分けて一陣の風が吹き抜けていく様と、そのときの自然の息吹にふれた感動が、表現者としての彼女の原風景になったのだという。自分の制作姿勢について語る彼女のことばは簡潔でやさしい。「私は私が見たいもの、今までに見たことのないものを作りたいと思います」。このことばから、私は、「詩とは、見えないものを見たい、聞こえないものを聞きたい、触れないもの触りたい、嗅げないもの嗅ぎたい、味わえないものを味わいたい、感じられないものを感じたい、無いものをあらしめたい、という願望

のことです」と語る詩人、宗左近の詩についての記述を想い起こした。

　この「詩」は、「音楽」にも、「美術」にも、およそ芸術といわれるもののすべてに置き換えることができるだろう。しかし、自分の願望を造形化するのはたやすいことではない。どれだけの詩人が、音楽家が、美術家が、苦悩し挫折を繰り返したことだろうか。精神を研ぎすまし、自分の心の源泉を豊かに潤し、その表現手段を、忍耐強く模索しなければならない。それを手に入れたものだけが夢を可能にする特権を与えられてきたのである。

　熊井恭子は、1983年、ステンレス・スティール線を自分の夢を託す素材として積極的に選び取ったときに、この特権を手に入れた。東京芸術大学ヴィジュアル・デザイン科を卒業した後、彼女は独学で織りを学び、1975年には色彩豊かな立体的な織造形作品を日本クラフト展に出品して新人賞を受賞しているのだが、この作品を見ると、何が彼女を織りに向かわせたのかが理解できるような気がする。縦糸と緯糸の織り目にすでに空気を潜ませて空間に浮遊する可塑性に富んだ織り布が生み出す立体的な造形に、彼女は自分の心を捉えて離さない大気の表現の可能性を期待したのであろう。しかし柔軟な布は重力に支配されるという宿命を負わされ、その造形には制約がある。また私たちの体を包み、飾り、生活を彩ってきた繊維素材のぬくもりは、自然のおおらかな包容力を伝えてはくれても、熊井が感動した風の息吹や大気のきらめく鮮烈さは表現しにくかったのかもしれない。重力から自立した織り布、空間に風の息吹を呼び覚ます緊張感に富んだ繊細かつ強靱な布を熊井は求めた。そして、1976年、ステンレス・スティール線が登場する。

Air NY

1991

stainless steel filament

11.2 x 21 x 45ft (3.5 x 6.5 x 14m)

Projects 28, Kyoko Kumai at

Museum of Modern Art, New York

Curator: Matilda McQuaid

Courtesy of Museum of Modern Art, New York

この段階ではまだそれは形態を重力から解放するための支持体であったが、ステンレス・スティール線の経糸に支えられて熊井の作品は生命を吹き込まれたように風をはらんで空間に飛び出した。彼女の風が空間に吹き始めたのである。しかし、彼女の心の中でより深く細やかになっていく自然観は、既成の素材と織技法ではもはや実現しがたくなっていたのだろう。やがてステンレス・スティール線は、彼女の願望を伝える重要なことばとして徐々に表舞台に姿を現し、経糸も緯糸もすべてステンレス・スティールの、きらめく織り布となり、ついには織機から離れ始めた。1983年のことであった。

彼女の身内からわき上がる感動が体中を駆け抜けて、手を通して直接にステンレス・スティール線に伝えられるようになった時、彼女の表現の語彙は飛躍的に豊かになった。ついに夢を現実にする特権を手に入れたのである。クレタのミダス王の手に触れたものがまたたくうちに金に変わったように、彼女の手を通してステンレス・スティール線は光をはらんだ大気となった。こうして風が、霧が、雨が、雪が、炎が、思いもかけないほど大胆に、そして繊細に、衝撃的な姿で私たちの前に立ち現れることとなった。高度な最先端技術が生み出した工業用のステンレス・スティールの細く強靱で無機的な線が、私たちの生命の根源ともいえる大自然に変わり得ると誰が思ったことだろう。

Screen – D
1987
stainless steel filament
9.6 x 4.2ft (3 x 1.3m)

《AIR CUBE》の支配する空間の中で私は懐かしい安らぎを感じた
と書いたが、それはその時一瞬、桃山時代の水墨画の名作、長谷川等
伯の《松林図屏風》を見たように思ったからだった。渺々と広がる余
白の中に数本の松の木が絶妙な間合いでリズミカルに配置された、墨
の濃淡だけが作り出す簡素な画面ではあるが、そこには光を含んだ煙
雨が立ちこめる無限の空間が広がり、松の葉音が静かな余韻を響かせ
て聞こえてくるような気がする。濃く薄く無限のヴァリエーションを
見せて銀色にきらめく《AIR CUBE》の支配する空間は、この《松林
図屏風》にどこか通じる、私たちを包み込んで悠久の時空間に運ぶ豪
奢な静謐感に満ちていた。

　いずれの時代でも、革新的な作品はいつも充実した過去の蓄積の中
から生まれてきた。熊井が生み出す現代の息吹を伝える風の中には、
自然に限りない信頼を寄せて自分の心の世界を投影し一体化していく
日本古来の自然観と、生命力に満ちた華麗な装飾性と簡素な静謐感が
表裏一体となって溶け合った日本文化の根底をなす美意識が、しっか
りと包みこまれている。《AIR CUBE》を前にして私が感じた懐かし
さや安らぎはここに起因するのだろう。

　最近の熊井は《叢生》のタイトルのもとに冬枯れの草むらをイメー
ジした作品に取り組んでいる。生命の最後の輝きを映したような淡く
柔らかな光の中に寂寥感が惻々と迫ってくる作品からは、自然の循環
のうちに人間の生死までも抱きとめようとするかのような作者の暖か
く静かなまなざしが窺われる。自然の息吹にふれた感動から表現者と
して出発した熊井は、より自在となった語彙を駆使して、いま世界の
本質にまで分け入ろうとしているのだろうか。

※本文中の「AIR CUBE」は常設展示ではありません。

Colour Plates

A Beginning – C
2001
stainless steel filament
8 x 8 x 8in (20 x 20 x 20cm)

Windy Earth in the Morning (left)
Windy Earth in the Night (above)
1990
stainless steel filament
3.2 x 32 x 64ft (1 x 10 x 20m)
Installation at Ohara-Ryu Kaikan, Tokyo

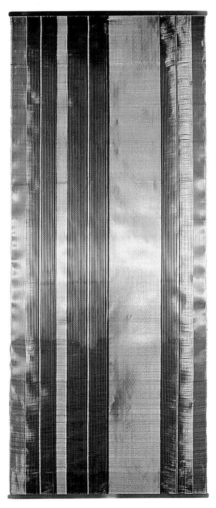

left:

SCREEN-V
1987
stainless steel filament
9.6 x 4.2ft (3 x 1.3m)

right:

Wind fom Clouds 1992
stainless steel filament
6.4 x 9.6 x 0.3ft (2 x 3 x
0.1m)
Collection of Museum of
Modern Art, New York

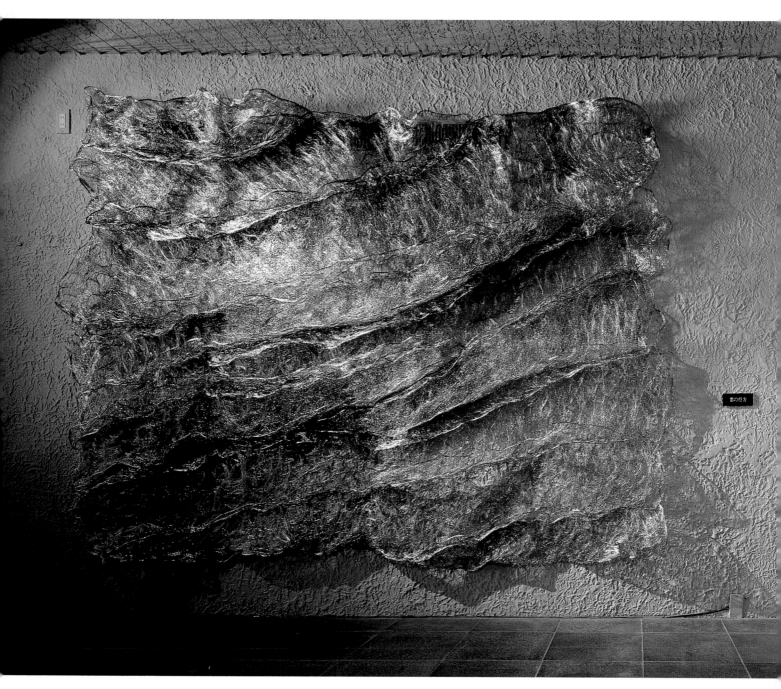

left:

Sen Man Na Yu Ta – Ebisu
1994
stainless steel filament, metal frame
17 x 14 x 2.6ft (5.4 x 4.5 x 0.8m)
commissioned by and installed at Ebisu
Garden Place, Tokyo

right:

Sen Man Na Yu Ta – Ga
1996
stainless steel filament
9.6 x 12.8 x 9.6ft (3 x 4 x 3m)

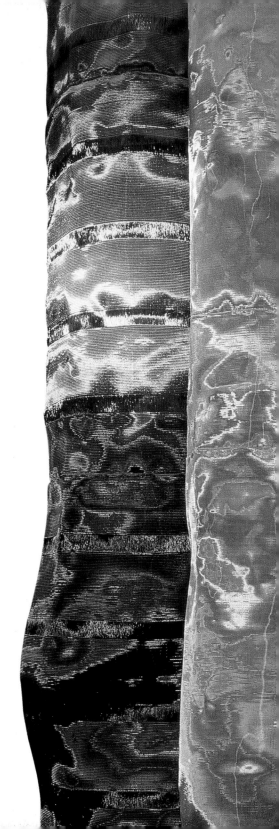

Flame

1990

stainless steel filament

9.6 x 32 x 2.2ft (3 x 10 x 0.7m)

Commissioned by Tokyo-Budoukan

above:

The Air '85 (detail)

1985

stainless steel filament

2.2 x 32 x 32ft (0.7 x 10 x 10m)

right:

A Beginning – S

2001

stainless steel filament

7.6in Ø (20cm)

Biography

Born	1943, Tokyo

Education and Awards

1962 -66	Tokyo National University of Fine Arts & Music
1975	New Talent Prize, Japan Craft Design Exhibition
1983	Excellence Prize, Japan Craft Design Exhibition
1986	Grand Prix, Kyushu Craft Design Exhibition, Japan
1987	New Technology and Kyoto Governor's Prize;
	1st International Textile Competition
1989	Asahi Gendai Craft Exhibition, Japan
1998	Bronze Medal: 9th International Tapestry Triennial, Lodz, Poland

Work in Collection

Savaria Museum, Hungary

Musée des Arts Décoratifs de Montréal, Canada

Museum of Modern Art, New York, USA

Ohita Prefectural Art Museum, Japan

Victoria & Albert Museum, London

Ashikaga City Art Museum, Japan

Science Museum, London

Central Museum of Textiles, Lodz, Poland

Oita City Art Museum, Japan

Gunma Prefectural Museum of Modern Art, Japan

Musée de Textiles, Angers, France

North Dakota Museum of Art, USA

Selected Solo Exhibitions

2002	'Wind Blowing over the Grass', C-square of Chukyo University, Nagoya
1999	'Kyoko Kumai Works', Contemporary Art, NIKI, Tokyo
1998	SOHSEI Gallery Space 21, Wacoal Ginza Art Space, Sembikiya Gallery. Tokyo
1996	'Air', Gallery Gallery, Gallery Maronie, Kyoto
1992	Sen Man Na Yu Ta, Itohchi Art Stage, Tokyo
1991	Projects 28 Kyoko Kumai, Museum of Modern Art, New York
1990	'Fiber Works', Plus Minus Gallery, Tokyo
1988	'Air', Gallery Gallery, Kyoto
1987	'Silver Rush', Oita Prefectural Art Museum, Oita
1985	'Blowing in The Wind', Striped House Art Museum, Tokyo
1983	'Blowing in the Wind', Oita Prefectural Art Museum, Oita

Selected Group Exhibitions

2001	'Textural Space – Contemporary Japanese Textile Art', Foyer Gallery, Farnham, UK (tour)
	10th International Tapestry Triennial, Lodz, Poland, member of the Jury
2000	'1st Echigo Tsumari Art Triennial', Niigata
1999	'Contemporary Art of Linear Construction', Yokohama Museum of Art, Yokohama
1998	9th International Tapestry Triennial, Lodz, Poland
1997-02	'Challenge of Materials', Science Museum, London
1995	'Japanese Fiber Arts', Victoria & Albert Museum London
1994-97	'Textiles and New Technology 2010', UK (tour: the Netherlands)
1992	6th International Textile Competition, Kyoto, member of the Jury
1987-91	1st, 2nd, 3rd, 5th International Textile Competition, Kyoto
1987	13th Lausanne International Tapestry Biennial, Switzerland

Selected Publications and Reviews

2001	'Textural Space', exhibition catalogue, edited by Lesley Millar
1999	*The Contemporary Arts of Linear Construction*, edited by Eiko Numata
1995	'Lights and Winds: Junichi Arai and Kyoko Kumai', exhibition catalogue, essay by Kiyoshi Ejiri
	Japanese Studio Crafts, edited by Rupert Faulkner
1994	*Textiles and New Technology, 2010*, edited by Sarah Braddock and Marie O'Mahony
	International Crafts, edited by Martina Margetts
	Fiber Arts Japan, edited by Kiyoji Tsuji
1991	*Monthly Atelier*, August, 'Moma Projects 28: Kyoko Kumai', essay by the Editor
	The New York Times, May 10, 'A Weaving of Stainless Steel Thread', essay by Roberta Smith
	The Brochure of Moma, Projects 28, 'The Works of Kyoko Kumai 1975 - 1990', essay by Matilda McQuaid
1990	Ginka Summer, 'Fiber works Now-weaving Images and Dreams', essay by Hideko Tahara
1989	*Sculpture*, May, 'The Many Forms of Fiber', essay by Janet Koplos
	Monthly Advance, Oita, January, 'Fabrics of Kyoto Kumai', essay by Shoko Miura
1988	*Monthly Atelier* 739, 'Fiber as the Front Technique of Expression'
	Design no Genba 28, 'Artists of space', essay by Kohichi Demura
1987	*Monthly Shitsunai*, December, 'Experiments of Fiber'
1986	*Monthly Senshoku-a*, May, 'New Materials and the Works', essay by Kyoko Kumai
	Axis 18, 'Images and Works of Kyoko Kumai', essay by Yasuko Seki